EXPLORING OUR
UNIVERSE

GALAXIES

HEATHER C. HUDAK

Checkerboard
Library

An Imprint of Abdo Publishing
abdopublishing.com

abdopublishing.com

Published by Abdo Publishing, a division of ABDO, PO Box 398166, Minneapolis, Minnesota 55439. Copyright ©2017 by Abdo Consulting Group, Inc. International copyrights reserved in all countries. No part of this book may be reproduced in any form without written permission from the publisher. Checkerboard Library™ is a trademark and logo of Abdo Publishing.
Printed in the United States of America, North Mankato, Minnesota
102016
012017

THIS BOOK CONTAINS RECYCLED MATERIALS

Design: Emily O'Malley, Mighty Media, Inc.
Production: Mighty Media, Inc.
Editor: Paige Polinsky
Cover Photograph: NASA
Interior Photographs: Alamy, p. 17 (bottom); Getty Images, p. 25; Mighty Media, Inc., p. 18; NASA, pp. 6, 7, 8, 9, 11, 16, 19, 21, 23, 27, 29; Shutterstock, pp. 5, 13; Wikimedia Commons, pp. 14, 17 (top), 26

Publisher's Cataloging-in-Publication Data

Names: Hudak, Heather C., author.
Title: Galaxies / by Heather C. Hudak.
Description: Minneapolis, MN : Abdo Publishing, 2017. | Series: Exploring our universe | Includes bibliographical references and index.
Identifiers: LCCN 2016944829 | ISBN 9781680784046 (lib. bdg.) | ISBN 9781680797572 (ebook)
Subjects: LCSH: Galaxies--Juvenile literature.
Classification: DDC 523.1/12--dc23
LC record available at http://lccn.loc.gov/2016944829

CONTENTS

MISSION
MILKY WAY

Many stars dot the clear night sky. Scientists believe there are more than 100 billion **trillion** in the universe. Each of these many stars belongs to a galaxy.

Billions of Galaxies

There are many different galaxies. Scientists think there are 100 billion in our universe. Along with stars, each galaxy contains planets, moons, and other celestial bodies.

Right at Home

Earth is part of the Milky Way galaxy. So are its neighboring planets and the sun. But our solar system is just one of many. Scientists have found 500 other solar systems in the Milky Way. They expect to find billions more.

Our galaxy, the Milky Way, contains about 100 billion stars.

Big Beyond Belief

The Milky Way galaxy is huge. Scientists believe it contains 17 billion Earth-sized planets! Its neighboring galaxy, Andromeda, is even bigger. Andromeda is more than 2.5 million **light-years** from our galaxy. But on clear, dark nights, you can see it with the naked eye.

CHAPTER 1

WHAT IS A GALAXY?

A galaxy is a huge group of stars, gas, dust, and planets held together by gravity. There are three main types of galaxies. They are spiral, elliptical, and irregular. Most galaxies seen from Earth are spiral galaxies.

A spiral galaxy has a dense bulge of stars at its center. More stars spiral out like long arms. This gives the galaxy a pinwheel shape. Newer stars are found in a spiral galaxy's outer arms. Older stars are closer to the center.

A barred galaxy is a type of spiral galaxy. A bar-shaped group of stars **spans** the center of each barred galaxy. More stars spiral out from this bar. The Milky Way galaxy is barred.

Scientists believe about one-third of spiral galaxies are barred.

All of the stars in a spiral galaxy orbit the galaxy's center.

Giant elliptical galaxies never have many young stars.

    The largest galaxies in our universe are elliptical. These galaxies are made of old stars with very little gas or dust. Elliptical galaxies range from round to oval shaped. Unlike other galaxies, they have no bars or arms. The stars in an elliptical galaxy do not orbit the galaxy's center. They have **random** paths.

Fewer elliptical galaxies are visible to us on Earth. For this reason, they are lesser known. But scientists think nearly half of all galaxies are elliptical.

Galaxies that have no real shape are called irregular. They are typically smaller than other galaxies. Irregular galaxies are made of new stars and large amounts of gas and dust. Only about 3 percent of all galaxies are irregular.

DID YOU KNOW ?

Many scientists believe large galaxies have black holes at their centers. A black hole forms when an enormous amount of matter packs into a tiny space. This would be like cramming 13 million Earths into New York City!

Scientists once believed NGC 5408 was a cloud of old star material. They now know it's an entire elliptical galaxy!

CHAPTER 2

THE BIRTH OF GALAXIES

The first galaxies formed about 13 billion years ago.
The universe was already a few hundred million years old.
Back when the universe formed, its temperatures were
extremely high. It was too hot for certain gases to exist.

After a few hundred thousand years, the universe
cooled down. This cooling created an atmosphere where
the elements **hydrogen** and **helium** could form. Together,
these elements formed large gas clouds. Some small
pieces of the clouds were denser
than others. Gravity caused
these pieces to collapse and
cool, forming the first stars.
Eventually, the first
stars exploded. The debris
then created new star clusters.

DID YOU KNOW ?

When galaxies first began
to form, stars were born
ten times faster than they
are today.

Spiral galaxy M51 *(bottom)* merges with a smaller galaxy *(top)*.

Heat from the exploding stars caused the larger gas clouds to collapse. Over time, the gas clouds and star clusters came together to form galaxies.

The first galaxies **collided** and **merged**. They grew in size and changed shape. As the universe expanded, these new galaxies moved away from each other.

CHAPTER 3

A HISTORY OF DISCOVERY

Humans have long been fascinated with starry skies. Since ancient times, one hazy band of light was particularly mystifying. We now know this is the Milky Way. But ancient humans had other ideas.

American Indians believed the Milky Way was a path for human souls. The Inca of Peru thought it was a river. They believed a thunder god used it to create rain. But the name Milky Way came from the ancient Greeks.

In Greek myths, the god Zeus had a son named Heracles. Zeus let Heracles drink milk from Zeus's wife, Hera, as she slept. When she moved away, the milk shot out of Heracles' mouth. This formed the Milky Way.

Early astronomers turned to science. They grouped stars into constellations. They mapped the movements of the sun and moon. But they often disagreed on facts.

Ancient Egyptians also compared our glowing galaxy to milk.
They believed the galaxy was the milk of a cow god.

Galileo (*center*) demonstrated his telescope to the high-ranking officials of Venice, Italy. They were so impressed that they doubled his salary.

In 5 BCE, Greek philosopher Democritus studied the Milky Way. He thought it was the light of distant stars. But Greek philosopher Aristotle disagreed. He said it was created by stars **igniting** inside Earth's atmosphere.

Persian and Islamic astronomers developed their own theories. They believed the Milky Way contained faraway star clusters. The truth was not known until much later.

In 1609, Italian scientist Galileo Galilei studied the sky with a telescope. He was the first person to do so. And he proved Aristotle wrong. Galileo confirmed that the Milky Way was made of distant stars.

The important galactic discoveries continued. In 1755, philosopher Immanuel Kant claimed the stars orbited a flat disk. Thirty years later, astronomer William Herschel made a map of this disk. He drew the Milky Way as a cloud-like mass of stars. Its center held the solar system.

Herschel's map was the first of its kind. But it was not perfect. Herschel did not realize gas and dust blocked parts of the Milky Way from view.

Modern technology has recorded our deepest ever view of the visible universe. This single image contains about 10,000 different galaxies!

In the early 1900s, US astronomer Edwin Hubble made a huge discovery. Hubble proved the Milky Way was not the only galaxy in existence. There was a lot more to our universe than anyone had ever imagined.

SUPER SCIENTIST
EDWIN HUBBLE

Edwin Hubble was born on November 20, 1889, in Marshfield, Missouri. In school, he earned a degree in astronomy. After graduating, Hubble began working at the Mount Wilson Observatory in Pasadena, California.

During this time, he found other galaxies beyond the Milky Way. He also discovered that galaxies expand. Hubble's research helped scientists grasp the vast size of our universe.

Hubble's work is considered some of the most important in scientific history. The world's most powerful space telescope, the Hubble Space Telescope, was named after him.

Edwin Hubble used Mount Wilson Observatory's Hooker telescope to prove his theories.

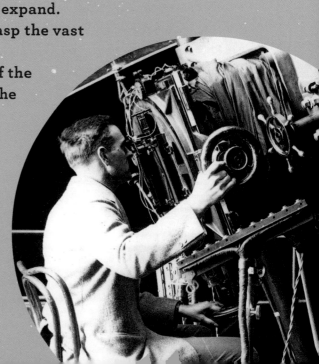

CHAPTER 4

MILKY WAY RESIDENTS

Scientists once thought the Milky Way contained the entire universe. Today, we know there are hundreds of billions of other galaxies. And many scientists believe our universe is not the only one.

Within the Milky Way galaxy is our solar system. Earth orbits the sun along with seven other planets. But the sun is just one of 200 billion Milky Way stars.

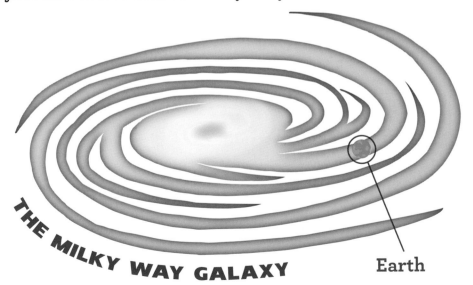

THE MILKY WAY GALAXY

Earth

No one knows for sure what the entire Milky Way looks like.
But artists and astronomers do their best to guess.

Scientists believe most stars have at least one planet. This means there are likely billions of planets beyond our solar system. These are called exoplanets. Most exoplanets are too far away to see or study.

CHAPTER 5

DIZZYING DARKNESS

The Milky Way has two main arms and two smaller arms. Its main arms are Scutum-Centaurus and Perseus. The minor arms are Sagittarius and Norma. Our own solar system lies in a small, partial arm called Orion. It is found between Sagittarius and Perseus.

But the Milky Way is more than spiraling arms. Within its disk, huge amounts of dust and hot gas mix with the stars. And at the very **core** of the Milky Way is a **black hole**. Black holes form when the most massive stars explode.

Our galaxy is also filled with dark matter. Scientists are not sure what makes up this dark matter. But they know it exists. Dark matter makes up about 90 percent of the Milky Way's entire mass. So only about 10 percent of the Milky Way can be seen from Earth.

A supermassive black hole rests at the Milky Way's core. This black hole's mass may be billions of times greater than our sun's mass.

CHAPTER 6

BEYOND THE MILKY WAY

Countless other galaxies lie beyond the Milky Way. Some are much larger than our own. Yet others are very small. Many dwarf galaxies have as few as 1,000 stars.

Most galaxies belong to a cluster. The smallest clusters have only a few galaxies. Others have thousands. Hot gas and dark matter fill the space between these galaxies. The clusters themselves are held together by gravity.

Clusters can be regular or irregular. Regular clusters are **spherical** and have more than 1,000 galaxies. Irregular clusters have fewer than 100 galaxies. These clusters don't have a specific shape. The galaxy we live in belongs to the irregular Local Group cluster.

DID YOU KNOW ?

Traveling at a speed of 200 miles per hour (322 kmh), it would take more than 7 trillion years to reach Andromeda.

An artist created this image of the Milky Way and Andromeda merging. This event likely won't happen for another 5 billion years.

The Milky Way is the second-largest galaxy in its cluster. It would take 100,000 **light-years** to travel across the galaxy lengthwise. Andromeda is even larger. Scientists believe the two galaxies will eventually **collide**. They will **merge** into one gigantic galaxy.

CHAPTER 7

STUDYING THE GALAXIES

We have come a long way from just staring up at the sky to study our galaxy. Today, scientists design spacecraft, such as **satellites** and **probes**. By sending these tools into space, they can gain a better understanding of our galaxy.

In 1957, Russia sent the first satellite into space. A few months later, the United States launched its own satellite. The satellites sent data back to Earth. They sent humans the first **extraterrestrial** view of the Milky Way.

This began the space race between Russia and the United States. Throughout the 1960s and 1970s, both countries sent humans and machines into orbit. Each mission gave us more data about our galaxy.

During this time, scientists considered sending a telescope into space. More than 20 years later, the European Space Agency (ESA) achieved that goal.

For four years, the telescope Hipparcos measured the position, motion, brightness, color, and distance of stars within our galaxy. Meanwhile, space agencies continued to build and improve **complex** spacecraft.

Moscow technicians record signals from Sputnik, the first satellite, in 1957.

In 1990, the National Aeronautics and Space Administration (**NASA**) launched the Hubble Space Telescope. It was the first major optical telescope placed in space. Nearly two decades later, NASA launched the Kepler Space Telescope. Its goal is to search for **habitable** Earth-sized planets in our galaxy.

In 2013, the ESA launched GAIA. This **satellite** will make a **3-D** map of the stars. Its goal is to better understand how the Milky Way formed.

Today's scientists are far from knowing everything about galaxies. But new tools will help us see deeper into space. We are on a nonstop journey of discovery. And with each finding, we will better understand the many galaxies in our universe.

On March 7, 2009, a Delta II rocket launched into space. It contained the Kepler Space Telescope.

TOOLS OF DISCOVERY

HUBBLE SPACE TELESCOPE

In 1990, NASA launched a telescope in Edwin Hubble's name. The Hubble Space Telescope (HST) orbits above Earth's atmosphere. It has recorded hundreds of thousands of images from this incredible position. These images have helped us understand the age of the universe, discover dark matter, and more.

The HST travels extremely fast. It could cross the entire United States in about ten minutes.

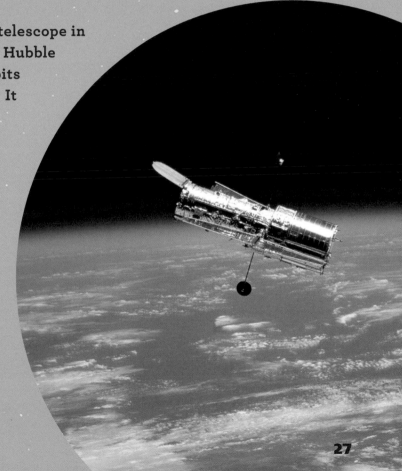

GALACTIC GUIDEBOOK

Milky Way

- Type: Barred Spiral
- Diameter: 100,000 light-years
- Placement of Earth: Orion arm

Centaurus A

- Type: Elliptical
- Distance from Earth: 13,000,000 light-years
- Diameter: 97,000 light-years

Andromeda

- Type: Spiral
- Distance from Earth: 2,500,000 light-years
- Diameter: 220,000 light-years

Hercules A

- Type: Elliptical with a supermassive black hole at the center
- Distance from Earth: 2,100,000,000 light-years
- Diameter: 1,500,000 light-years

Malin 1

- Type: Spiral (largest)
- Distance from Earth: 1,400,000,000 light-years
- Diameter: 650,000 light-years (outer disk)

Sombrero

- Type: Spiral with large bulge and dust ring
- Distance from Earth: 28,000,000 light-years
- Diameter: 50,000 light-years

The Tadpole

- Type: Spiral with long tail
- Distance from Earth: 420,000,000 light-years
- Diameter: 390,000 light-years

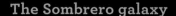

The Sombrero galaxy

GLOSSARY

black hole — an area of space where the gravity is so strong light cannot escape.

collide — to come together with force.

complex — having many parts, details, ideas, or functions.

core — the central part of a celestial body, usually having different physical properties from the surrounding parts.

diameter — the distance across the middle of an object such as a circle.

extraterrestrial — coming from beyond Earth.

habitable — safe and good enough for people to live in.

helium — a light, colorless gas that does not burn.

hydrogen — a gas with no smell or color that is lighter than air and catches fire easily.

ignite — to set on fire.

light-year — the distance that light travels in one year.

merge — to combine or blend.

NASA — National Aeronautics and Space Administration. NASA is a US government agency that manages the nation's space program and conducts flight research.

Persian — of or having to do with the present-day country of Iran.

probe — a device used to explore and send back information.

random — lacking a definite plan or pattern.

satellite — a manufactured object that orbits Earth. It relays scientific information back to Earth.

span — to reach over or stretch across something.

spherical (SFIHR-i-kuhl) — having a globe-shaped body.

3-D — having three dimensions, such as length, width, and height. Something that is three-dimensional appears to have depth.

trillion — the number 1,000,000,000,000, or one thousand billion.

WEBSITES

To learn more about Exploring Our Universe, visit booklinks.abdopublishing.com. These links are routinely monitored and updated to provide the most current information available.

INDEX